S0-EAY-874

Beavers

Christine Butterworth

Silver Burdett Press, Morristown, New Jersey

It is a hot summer day.
This beaver is hard at work.
He is cutting down trees
to make a dam.

He bites the trees with
his sharp yellow teeth.
Look at these tree stumps.
The trees have been
cut down by beavers.

The beaver works by a stream.
He needs the trees to make
a dam across the stream.
He cuts the trees into short logs.
He uses the logs to make the dam.

Another beaver comes to help.
She takes a log and
swims to the dam.
She puts the log into
the wall of the dam.

The beavers push mud around the logs
to keep them in place.
They put sticks on top of the dam.
Soon the dam is as high as a tall man.
The beavers use the dam to make a lake.

The water in the stream is
held back by the dam.
Soon the dam makes a deep lake.
Now the beavers can make their home.
Their home is called a lodge.

They cut down more trees
to make their lodge.
They make a pile of logs
in the middle of the lake.
They make two tunnels under
the water at the bottom of
the pile of logs.

8

The other ends of the tunnels
come up inside the lodge.
The beavers make a room in
the lodge where they can sleep.

The beavers are hungry after
all their hard work.
One beaver finds a stick and
chews the bark.
The other eats some
water lily leaves.

This beaver is resting in the sun
to dry his fur.
Beavers' coats are thick and soft.
Their tails have no fur, though.
They are wide and flat.

The beavers comb their fur
with their claws.
They swim back to their lodge and
sit on top of it.
They do not see the bear
on the shore of the lake.

The bear is looking for food.
A beaver in the water sees the bear.
The beaver smacks the water with
its flat tail. Slap!
The sound tells other beavers
that there is danger nearby.

There is a slide built on
the side of the lodge.
The beavers slide down it. Splash!
They dive deep under the water.
They go into their lodge
to hide from the bear.

14

Beavers can swim fast underwater.
They find the way into the lodge.
The tunnel is deep under the water.
Other animals cannot get in.
The bear cannot catch the beavers now.

One beaver is hungry.

He takes some leaves to eat when

he swims to the lodge.

He swims into the tunnel.

He climbs into the room inside the lodge.

The beaver will be safe in the lodge.

The bear looks at the beaver lodge
in the middle of the lake.
It can smell the beavers,
but it cannot get into the lodge.
The bear goes away.
The beavers stay inside the lodge.

Now it is winter.
The lake is frozen.
Snow covers the beaver home.
The beaver family rests
inside the lodge.

18

Beavers do not sleep
all the time in the winter.
They wake up when they are hungry.
There is a pile of logs and
sticks near the lodge.
This is the beavers' food supply.

19

The tunnel to the lodge
is deep under the water.
The tunnel does not freeze.
The beavers can leave the lodge
to get sticks from their food supply.

These beavers are climbing back
into their sleeping room in the lodge.
Soon the male beaver will mate
with the female beaver.
She will wait for sixteen weeks
to have her babies.

Spring has come.
The snow and ice melt.
The female beaver will soon
have her babies.

The young beavers born last year
are growing big.
Soon the mother and father beaver
will send them away.
They need room in the lodge
for the new babies.

The mother beaver has her babies.

They have thick, soft fur.

Each one is the size of a small cat.

After a week the mother takes
her babies out of the lodge.
See how well they can swim.
They follow her to
the edge of the lake.

A hungry wild dog smells the babies.
The mother beaver growls and
shows her sharp teeth.
She scares the wild dog away.

26

The baby beavers grow bigger.
They help to fix the dam.
The dam must be strong
to keep the water in the lake.

Summer is over.
The leaves turn red and yellow.
The beavers put more mud
on their lodge.
They must make the roof strong.
Winter is coming.

This young beaver wants
a lodge of his own.
He finds a good place in the lake.

The young beaver cuts sticks
with his teeth.
He makes a big pile of sticks and
mud in the lake.
He makes a tunnel into the lodge.

Inside the lodge, the beaver has made
his sleeping room.
He has chewed the ends off the sticks.
He has lined the room with dry grass.
Now he has a warm, dry home.

A female beaver joins him.
They swim out to the lodge.
In the winter they will be warm and
safe inside the lodge.

Reading consultant: Diana Bentley
Editorial consultant: Donna Bailey

Illustrated by Paula Chasty
Picture research by Suzanne Williams
Designed by Richard Garratt Design

First published in 1988 by
Macmillan Children's Books,
a division of Macmillan Publishers Limited
4 Little Essex Street, London WC2R 3LF and Basingstoke

Published in the United States by
Silver Burdett Press, Morristown, New Jersey.

Printed in Hong Kong

Library of Congress Cataloging-in-Publication Data
Butterworth, Christine.
   Beavers.
   (My world)
   Summary: Describes how beavers build dams and
lodges, find food, mate, give birth, and evade
predators.
   1. Beavers——Juvenile literature.   [1. Beavers]
I. Chasty, Paula, ill.   II. Title.   III. Series:
Butterworth, Christine.   My world.
QL737.R632B88   1988   599.32′32   87-23458
ISBN 0-382-09555-3

Photographs
Cover: Zefa
Bruce Coleman: 3, 5 and 6 (Leonard Lee Rue), 7 (Jonathan
   Wright), 10 (James Simon), 13 (Hans Reinhard), 20 (Leonard
   Lee Rue), 21 (Jen & Des Bartlett), 22 (Wayne Lankinen), 25
   (Jen & Des Bartlett), 26 (James Simon), 27 (Wayne Lankinen),
   32 (James Simon)
Frank Lane Picture Agency: 2 (K. Maslowski), 4 (Mark
   Newman), 11 (K. Maslowski), 17 (Mark Newman), 30 (S.
   McCutcheon)
Survival Anglia: 23 (Bomford & Borkowski), 24 and 31 (Jen & Des
   Bartlett)
Zefa: titlepage, 12, 16